Penguin Modern Europe[an]
Advisory Editor: A. Alva[rez]

Selected Poems · A[bba]

Abba Kovner was born at Sevastopol in the Crimea, in 1918, and grew up in Vilna, where he graduated at the Hebrew Gymnasium. He played a leading part in the Zionist youth movement, and shortly before the war published his first poem in a local Hebrew journal. After the Nazi invasion he joined the Jewish underground partisan organization, the P.P.O., and shortly before the extermination of the Vilna ghetto, led a band of fighters into the neighbouring forests. In 1946 he settled in a kibbutz in Palestine and became an Israeli citizen in 1948. Kovner has always written in Hebrew. In 1968 he won the Brenner Literary Prize, and in 1970 the Israeli Prize for Literature.

Nelly Sachs was born in Berlin in 1891. She began writing verses at the age of seventeen but, although some were published, she remained virtually unrecognized. When the Nazis came to power she lived in isolation, taking refuge in the works of the German and Jewish mystics, who greatly influenced her poetry. In 1940, at the last possible moment, she escaped to Sweden. There she found her mature poetic voice, combining the inspiration of the German masters Hölderlin and Rilke with that of surrealism and the Old Testament. She wrote in German, and in 1966 received the Nobel Prize for Literature. She died in 1970.

Selected Poems

Abba Kovner

Translated by
Shirley Kaufman and
Nurit Orchan

Nelly Sachs

Translated by
Michael Hamburger,
Ruth and Matthew Mead,
and Michael Roloff
Selected by
Stephen Spender

With an Introduction by Stephen Spender

Penguin Books

Penguin Books Ltd, Harmondsworth,
Middlesex, England
Penguin Books Australia Ltd, Ringwood,
Victoria, Australia

Published in Penguin Books 1971

My Little Sister by Abba Kovner, originally
published in Hebrew, under the title *Achoti Ktana*, by
Sifriat Poalim, Tel Aviv, Israel, 1967, copyright
© Abba Kovner, 1967.
The poems by Nelly Sachs are taken from *Fahrt
ins Staublose*, copyright © Suhrkamp Verlag,
Frankfurt am Main, 1962; *Späte Gedichte*, copyright ©
Suhrkamp Verlag, Frankfurt am Main, 1965.
Translations first published in *Nelly Sachs:
Selected Poems*, copyright © 1967 by Farrar,
Straus and Giroux Inc., first published in Great
Britain by Jonathan Cape, 1968.

Made and printed in Great Britain by
Hazell Watson & Viney Ltd
Aylesbury, Bucks
Set in Monotype Bembo

Contents

Introduction

Communism, wrote Marx and Engels, was a spectre haunting nineteenth-century Europe. The events of the twentieth century are less ghostly; they have loaded Europe with real corpses: the victims of Stalin's purges and of the Nazi gas chambers, the dead of two world wars. It would be wrong to suggest that European and American poets have not reacted to these massacres. But they have reacted, for the most part, not directly to the horrific facts, but indirectly, to their effects on the general condition of the culture. The agony of the 'hooded hordes swarming / Over endless plains' has appeared as the fragmentation of civilization, the breakdown of traditional values. The idea of the death of millions of people being a subject for poetry threatens a tradition in which tragedy concentrates on the suffering of one symbolic, exalted victim – the crucified hero – with whom audience or readers identify and in whom they recognize their own deepest sense of what is terrible. For there to be tens of thousands of tragic heroes would be to submerge Oedipus, Hamlet and Lear in massive anonymity; and the anonymous victim is, in the Western tradition, no subject for tragedy. For this reason certain poets in central Europe who survived the destruction of cities and the horrors of concentration camps have agreed with T. W. Adorno that 'after Auschwitz' poetry can no longer be written.

There are reasons within the tradition itself why European and American poets should see, in the direct confrontation of poetic imagination with the most terrible realities of the contemporary world, the destruction of all the standards whereby poetry has continued to be written.

However, there are also reasons why, within the quite different Jewish tradition, poets such as Nelly Sachs and Abba Kovner can write poetry about the massacre of millions of their compatriots in the gas chambers without appearing to think that this is material unsuitable for poetry, or that their poems depict a 'waste land' of despair and the end of civilization, or that what they are writing is 'anti-poetry'.

In suggesting that these two Jewish poets draw upon the same tradition, I do not mean to imply that their work is similar. Within that tradition they are unalike both in background and in what they write.

Nelly Sachs was born in Berlin in 1891, and began in the German romantic vein of Goethe and Schiller. Only after Hitler came to power did she turn to the Jewish cabala for a model. 'Book and inscription, archive and alphabet: these are concepts that recur throughout her work,' wrote Hans Magnus Enzensberger in his introduction to her *Selected Poems.* When she fled to Sweden in 1940 she continued to write in German.

Abba Kovner comes from an entirely Jewish Eastern European background, where Hebrew was the language spoken by his family. His Polish childhood, his wartime youth – as a very young man he and four friends organized the Jewish resistance to the German occupation of Vilna – and his career as a soldier and poet writing in Israel, are all exclusively and consistently Jewish.

But both poets have in common the tradition of the Old Testament, which is utterly different from that of the Latin, Greek and Christian West and affects their work in an utterly different way. For western readers, the contrast between the Jewish and the European traditions may throw light on the problems facing modern poets in the age of great massacres and the holocaust. In the Old Testament, poetry is not an end in itself but the realization in language of a vision of life as old as the nation's history. Thus the traditional Jewish poet/prophet does not write simply as an individual artist expressing his exceptional sensibility for the benefit of other individuals. Instead, he is the voice of the people, a people for whom nationhood is religion and the individual but a fraction of the nation's millennial consciousness. His purposes are didactic and mystical, not aesthetic.

The lives most vividly present in the work of Nelly Sachs and Abba Kovner are those of the murdered. That is not to say that there is any gratuitous horror in their poetry, any Jacobean piling of corpses on corpses. They transform their material, spiritualizing it, but not in ways which make it any the less terrible. Horror, one might say, is turned in their work into the extreme agony of death-bed prayer, more terrifying but also calmer and more final than the gross fact. The poetry seems a veil between us and the dead. Metaphors of smoke and butterflies in Nelly Sachs, of ladders and chestnut trees in Abba Kovner, are mysterious, ascending, evanescent. Nelly Sachs writes:

> Butterfly
> blessed night of all beings!
> The weights of life and death
> sink down with your wings
> on the rose
> which withers with the light ripening homewards.

> What lovely aftermath
> is painted in your dust.
> What royal sign
> in the secret of the air.

Within the Old Testament tradition the poet is prophet and witness of the Jewish religious and national vocation.

Within the European tradition he is an individualist writing for other individualists. For the Jews, there is the fear that the individual will develop a consciousness isolated from that of the nation: the Jewish people, with their sense of being chosen, in the covenant and in suffering, have a consciousness which differs from the nationalism of any other nation, as it differs also from collectivist or proletarian class-consciousness. For people in the European tradition, there is the opposite fear of a Dark Age in which there will no longer be individuals – no outstanding creators and spirits capable of independently cultivating themselves.

Greek, Christian, Renaissance and modern tragedy all project the deepest feelings and imaginative life of each member of the audience on to the hero. The hero is traditionally exempt, by superior birth and possessions, from the poverty and misery which make the average person liable to ordinary misfortune. His position stresses a uniqueness which corresponds to the uniqueness within every member of the audience considered individually and alone. The hero endures an idealized suffering which strikes responsive chords in the deepest, most isolated consciousness of every member of the audience. Therefore if, as has happened in our time, tens of thousands of people are made objects of torment by some, and of pity for others, the principle of European Aristotelian tragedy is undermined. The massacres demand either that we should regard the victims as an anonymous abstraction (as Eliot does in *The Waste Land*), or that we should regard each one of them as a hero. In either case the European tradition risks being thrown into extreme attitudes. Certain poets find aristocratic or Nietzschean grounds for ignoring the suffering of the 'hooded hordes'. Yeats thought that poetry should dance over the graves of the dead. The refusal of traditionalists to imagine so much suffering makes them appear inhuman in the eyes of the members of a younger generation who have witnessed the slaughter and destruction. Yet an attempt to envisage thousands of victims as tragic heroes and heroines is too great a strain on the survivors, and, in art, risks becoming insincere. Thus the anguish of the massacred becomes, in terms of the European tradition, symptomatic of the breakdown of the culture. The victims become, among others, those 'objective forces' which, in Yeats's metaphorical system of the 'phases of the moon', blot out human individuality at the end of a cycle of civilization.

The Greek and New Testament tradition focuses always on the solitary figure of the sacrificial victim, the Hanged Man, Christ, or Oedipus. Thus the poet cannot make a tragedy out of a disaster which affects millions of people. Indeed, in this connection 'people' means the working classes, the man in the street, the social unit, the bourgeois, or, most poignantly, the soldiers in the trenches. However much these may be regarded as objects of pity, they are also below that level of cultivated self-awareness which would make them capable of tragedy. If one of them – a Jude the Obscure – is depicted by an author as tragic, this is because he is already a secret hero and his obscurity is ironic. When socialists talk of a future in which the people will rule, they mean that the people will all have become individuals.

Tragedy, in the poetry of Nelly Sachs and Abba Kovner, is the tragedy of the Jewish nation in all its history – not just of their contemporaries, not even just of the exterminated. By this I do not mean that there is no feeling for individual persons. Abba Kovner's fragile 'little sister' is individual, but, confined in the convent among the Christian nuns, she belongs to 'another god', another people. Nelly Sachs gives us the most intimate feeling of a loved person in 'If

I Only Knew', and yet both feeling and person dissolve
into the situation which is that of all victims:

> If I only knew
> On what your last look rested.
> Was it a stone that had drunk
> So many last looks that they fell
> Blindly upon its blindness?
>
> Or was it earth,
> Enough to fill a shoe,
> And black already
> With so much parting
> And with so much killing?

'Shoe' signifies those shoes, thousands of which the
visitor still sees collected at Auschwitz, the shoes in which
children and adults came to the camps and which were
collected from them before they entered the gas chambers,
the shoes that walked across the desert, the shoes that
carried the Jews from their contemporary world into the
universe of their history.

For us, such poetry bears witness to the plain fact that
Hitler's 'final solution' achieved an effect opposite to that
which he intended: it destroyed millions of individuals but
it resurrected them within the consciousness of the nation.
Abba Kovner writes:

> Our father took his bread, bless God,
> forty years from one oven. He never imagined
> a whole people could rise in the ovens
> and the world, with God's help, go on.

There have been many attempts before to wipe the Jews
off the face of the earth. This was the most recent, and if it
was also the most terrible, that was because the resources
of modern science enabled it to be. The inexpressibly,

incomprehensibly hideous events of this time and place paradoxically demonstrated the continuity of the Jews, their special fate and vocation. In the poetry of Nelly Sachs and Abba Kovner the Jews become again what they always were, the people of exile, of the pogroms and persecutions, of the diaspora and the homecoming, of the covenant and the promise.

It would be frivolous to suggest that for this reason the 'final solution' was a blessing in disguise. To say this would be to contradict the nature of tragedy. For tragedy is real death; and though an idea may be reborn from it with a sacred joy this does not make the destruction less complete. Despair and hope, sacrifice and promise, exist side by side in Jewish history, each equally real, irreconcilable opposites. In her 'Chorus of the Rescued' Nelly Sachs expresses this paradox of meeting which is also leave-taking.

> We, the rescued,
> We press your hand
> We look into your eye –
> But all that binds us together now is leave-taking,
> The leave-taking in the dust
> Binds us together with you.

Dust, like smoke, is a symbol of metamorphosis.

The non-Jewish reader may feel that in all this there is too much insistence on suffering, too remorseless and pressing a seriousness. One can only reply to such objections that to be a Jew has always been a serious matter. Suffering seems to be the chord that strikes the deepest note in Jewish consciousness. The view of life presented in the Old Testament is not, even in the Dantesque sense, a *commèdia*, any more than it is a Greek or a Shakespearean tragedy. The role of the Jews in the world's history has been to be conscious of nationhood in a way that no other nation has been, and with an intensity for which the word 'nationalism' is, at best, a vulgar parody. Nationhood in Jewish history means oneness of the people with God. And such consciousness of nationhood has left little room for anything else. It is to be hoped, perhaps, that there may be a Jewish future based on happiness in which Israel will break away from the cycle of suffering. Meanwhile, Jewish humour – of the kind that flickers in Abba Kovner's account of the Catholic nuns who show so little understanding of their Jewish sister – is not, like English humour, that of people who refuse to take themselves, or anyone else, seriously. It is the sparks that fly off the blade pressed to the grindstone.

The concept of poetry in the work of these two writers is not self-expression, nor confession, nor yet the invention of a self-sufficient artefact. It is, as I have said above, religious: but mystical rather than 'orthodox'. Nelly Sachs and Abba Kovner seek and discover metaphysical significance in suffering.

For the reasons I have given above, the poet in the European individualist tradition may be largely incapable of dealing directly with mass suffering. If he is subjective, his own personality and feelings, including his sympathy for others, will appear trivial when measured against the collective suffering of the victims. The suffering will seem a mockery, not only of his power to bear such an emotive burden, but of his concept of poetry. Each individual victim will seem a tragic hero, in the way Wilfred Owen, writing to Osbert Sitwell in 1918, described the men under his command on the Western Front:

> For 14 hours yesterday I was at work – teaching Christ to lift his cross by numbers, and how to adjust his crown; and not to imagine he thirst, until after the last halt.

Owen's own poetry retains its Keatsian richness, but his

subject matter mocks Keats's belief in a sensuous world of the imagination. The literal imagery of war parodies the richness of Romantic imagery: 'Heart, you were never hot, / Nor large, nor full like hearts made great with shot'; and 'Your slender attitude / Trembles not exquisite like limbs knife-skewed.' 'That's for your poetry book.' The real agony turns on the poetic agonizing and strangles it with bare hands. The poetry at best can be used as an ambulance to take the wounded to hospital. 'Above all,' writes Owen in his famous Preface, 'I am not concerned with poetry. My subject is war, and the pity of war. The poetry is in the pity.'

The reaction of Owen to mass suffering is to make each soldier a tragic hero, an object of pity and terror, with whom the poet identifies. The reaction of the young D. H. Lawrence to the war is almost the opposite of this. Instead of identifying with the suffering of the victims, Lawrence bitterly resents them, because they attack his own subjective consciousness which he stridently asserts against all those who accept the war, whether they are politicians or soldiers, English or Germans. In fighting and allowing themselves to be killed they have put themselves on the side of death; in refusing them sympathy, and being defiantly himself, he is on the side of life. Lawrence is not a pacifist, he has no pity for victims, he hates them for being killed and wounded and he rejects their implicit demand for sympathy. Although married to a German wife, he regarded the Germans as the prime instigators of all the hatred, and directed his own hatred particularly at them. He wrote to Lady Ottoline Morrell in 1915: 'I would like to kill a million Germans – two millions.' He forced out of his own consciousness that will to attain individuality which would reject the death lust of the surrounding civilization:

I will not live any more in this time. I know what it is. I reject it. As far as I possibly can, I stand outside this time, I will live my life, and, if possible, be happy, though the world slides in horror down into the bottomless pit.

Feeling the war to be a threat to his own individuality, he rejected the individuality of those fighting and fought his own private war to maintain the life in himself and a few others:

Nothing matters, in the end, but the little hard flame of truth one has inside oneself and which does not blow about in the draught of blasphemous living.

At the beginning of this introduction I mentioned the pronouncement of Professor T. W. Adorno that 'after Auschwitz' poetry could no longer be written. This pronouncement was echoed by certain young European and American poets, haunted by the victims, who judging contemporary poets by the continuance in their work of the heroic inhumanity or the self-destructive empathy of the surviving but fragmented European tradition, have written, programmatically, what they call 'anti-poems', and have renounced 'poetry' altogether. Here is a statement by the Polish poet Tadeusz Różewicz:

I cannot understand that poetry should survive when the men who created that poetry are dead. One of the premises and incentives for my poetry is a disgust with poetry. What I revolted against was that it had survived the end of the world, as though nothing had happened.

Nelly Sachs and Abba Kovner might reply to Różewicz that what they consider the end of the world is the beginning of poetry in the biblical tradition and has always been so. Różewicz goes on to say that he has fashioned his poems 'out of a remnant of words, salvaged words, out of uninteresting words, words from the great rubbish dump, the great cemetery'.

I have taken these two extracts from *The Truth of Poetry* by Michael Hamburger, who comments on them:

The 'great rubbish dump' and 'the great cemetery' are the realities to which the Second World War had reduced Różewicz and many other European poets.

Leaving aside Różewicz's deliberate tendentiousness, what is important is his feeling that 'after Auschwitz' poets should no longer write about their subjective feelings and that they should not create artefacts – aesthetic objects – out of language. 'The production of "beauty",' the same poet wrote in 1966, 'to induce "aesthetic experiences" strikes me as a harmless but ludicrous and childish occupation.' And he claims that he is writing 'for the horror-stricken. For those abandoned to butchery. For survivors. We learnt language from scratch, those people and I.'

While appreciating the sincerity of statements of this kind, one may demur at the conclusion that it is blasphemous for poets to go on writing 'as though nothing had happened'. Life does go on, and people will continue to explore themes of personal relations and the experiences of ordinary living. Nevertheless such statements do face us with the fact that concentration camps, bombings, forced transference of populations, etc., have shattered the bases of Renaissance individualist art which survived right up until 1939. The empathy of Wilfred Owen (a poet of whom the Polish writers may not have heard) and his cry of 'the poetry is in the pity' ends with horror and butchery flooding over the whole European tradition.

One turns then with special interest to poets such as Nelly Sachs and Abba Kovner who come from a civilization – a nation and a religion – with so different a conception of tragedy: tragedy as the awakening of the people – the Jewish people – to their national consciousness. Within the limits of this introduction it is impossible to speculate whether the threat of universal catastrophe today is not beginning to produce a world consciousness which is more communal than individualist, and whether this may not produce a poetry closer in attitude to that of the Jewish poets in this volume than to that of the great individualist poets who were writing in America and England early in the present century.

STEPHEN SPENDER

Abba Kovner

Translated from the Hebrew
by Shirley Kaufman and Nurit Orchan

Translators' Note

We wish to acknowledge the counsel of Dr Leib Schapiro and of Chana Faerstein Bloch and Professor Robert Alter, Department of Comparative Literature, University of California, Berkeley, whose suggestions were valuable in the translation of these poems. Professor Alter also assisted in the preparation of the notes.

We are grateful also to Professor Dan Miron of Tel Aviv University and T. Carmi of Jerusalem, who read and corrected the translation in Israel as it was interpreted to them by Abba Kovner.

SHIRLEY KAUFMAN and NURIT ORCHAN

My Little Sister

To Michael and Shlomit

They came as far as a wall.
On the seventh night into the dawn
heard from the wall the drowning in the snow
not seeing the marchers' faces
in the white wind.

Part One

I

Came as far as a wall. The iron ring
of the chime caught in a mass
of ice. They seized it, rubbed it
like holding the face of a frozen man.
Until the morning light
with invocations, with weeping nails;
begged the voice of the bell
to tear from the frost,
from the killing silence.
And the iron did not shake.
Nor tremble.

But we took with us the craziness
of a dog gnawing the moon in a puddle.
And it rang. One
awful ring. How is it
animals and birds inside the wall
did not freeze at this voice!
Nine sainted Sisters
hurried to the gate. Their voices withered.

Naked. Braids on her breast –
my fragile sister!*
Standing at the door.

My fragile sister: The 'little sister' of the title, an allusion to Song
of Songs, viii, 8, is connected here through an allusive pun to the
sister-bride invoked throughout the Song of Songs. The Hebrew
qallah can mean 'slight', 'quick', 'blithe', while *kallah* is 'bride'.
Combining the two meanings in English translation, the translators
chose 'fragile'.

3

My sister's eyes search the wall of the convent
for a scarlet thread. A candle trembles
in the nuns' hands.
Nine holy Sisters look at my sister

seeing – ashes that speak.

4

Dawn that wakes from fears. In light
wrenched from smoke, three chestnut trees
appear this morning
as if emerged from the land of the living:

my sister sees them close by.
My sister does not cry out. Only a catch
of joy in the throat. Nine nuns
are silent in black to my sister
like faces of monuments in a foreign city.

5
The bell rings six.
The Dominican Convent is awake.
The Sisters search my sister's eyes.
My fragile sister!
Nine Sisters look at you
uneasy

seeing – ashes that speak.

6

Angels go with my sister.
A flock of angels goes with my sister
as far as the doorway. My little sister!
She has taken another god,
a gate opens for her.

And a court.

7

Nine 'Little Sisters' in a gold frame
shining with inner light.
Doves ate
from their kissed hands.
When my dove came down at the foot of the wall,
torn wing,
their palms were gathered
in supplication,

pink as prayer beads, joints of their fingers
knock now,
while my sister stands at the door.

And the son sees
And the father stares.

8

A cloister's wall is high.
A wall of silence
still higher.
A ladder leans to a wall.
Tops of chestnut trees touch and recoil
from the bell tower.
Three chestnut trees
out of a land of lakes

and mud.

9

From here the world of the living
is seen.
From here a whole world watches
my face dissolve into
blue.

My sister is in the wall.
The waylayer at the gates.
In a heavy night robe,
in bare feet,
spying behind her back
god comes near.

The court is amazed. What yearning streams
through my land
– that bitch!

These starving eyes
ripe with love.
Silences
and velvet steps!
Such clean hands and pure minds!

From his suffering image,
from the feet of the cold statue,
look, with a delicate hand
dust is swept
into a gold coffer –
only my crucified memory
outside the fence!

In the court,
in a private language, my sister plays
with another god.

II

Walls of the house are bright.
No woman has crouched to give birth
on the floor.
No man screams
blood. Their beds
are made ready with pardons.
Small pardons drop
in the lap like a whore's pay.
And his light dripping warm.
If you will not come to us
– how shall we be consoled?

Night after night
the Sisters breathe hard in their beds
as if raised on a ladder.
Their bodies shake.
And on this night too, heavy with longing,
the gowns on their skins are burning.

In his high place,
quiet as a tree alone,
he stands.
And light of the mother and the father
trickles down from his face.

Then his bright body breaks out
of a gold frame.
Lord! He comes down
on a ladder of thorns.
His blood is not running.

He swings
in his thin limbs.

13

The granter of grace to the innocent
comes.
He arches over me, saying:
you are my daughter –
The sun.
The frost.
The heat.
All of them pierce my flesh.
His blazing forehead on my face
and the great sea in me.
No world but he.
None but he in me.

Only the soul is awake and knows
that this is the lust of knowing.

To give to love the
walkers in the snow. The
pressed. The
oppressor. All the
lost for they are lost.
To bring them back
in pity
in open arms
in ringing bells
in blood.

Nine Sisters drenched with pleasure.
Morning rises
for love.
My little sister
is scared.

15

The world that watched
withdrew,
Her beautiful doll,
father's gift,
they crushed in the snow.

No mother, no brother,
hands crossed over her growing breasts,
they waved my sister
through that gate.

Hid her within the wall.
With sainted patience
the ladies wait.
They are flooded with mercy.

My fragile sister!
No harbour – betrayal
– no island.
Only a folded sail in a storm.

Part Two

16
Far, far
A city lies. Body still warm.
Bells are ringing.

You have not seen a city thrust on its back
like a horse in its blood, jerking its hooves
unable to rise.

Bells are ringing.

City.
City.
How mourn a city
whose people are dead and whose dead are alive
in the heart.

Bells.

Now the Sisters are ready.
Ringing,

the bells chime their longing
into fixed rations,
into appointed times
for payment. And the wall keeps them
from the world.
Nine 'Little Sisters' pace in awe.
Their robes float. In procession.

My sister sits at the window. She
waits for a brother.

i
You never knew Vilk. He takes me
in his paws. He wets my eyes
with his warm tongue,
and when he says goodnight like this,
I hear my father's sandals
going to his rooms.

Tomorrow Vilk will carry me in his teeth,
and I will be like one of the whelps.

ii
One
bell for prayer.
A second bell
for danger.

A long rope hangs from one.
My sister's life
from the second.

Free of god,
the dog listens for the hidden bell
in the gate of the convent –
day and night.

iii
He never barks.
Before an alarm
he only bares his teeth,
and his eyes are filled with blood.

Then Vilk would set this creature gently

in the secrecy of the kennel. He would cover her face
with his hairy body,
and stand over her trembling. Mute.

When he was murdered, my sister washed Vilk
from head to foot
and wrote: my brother,
in the sand.

Christina is lame. She opens her day
with a murmur of eyelashes. Like a dove alarmed from
   its nest.
Christina circles his face,
a loose wing pleading.
Christina hazards her life
till he will take her to himself.

Christina knows there are endless ways,
but only one
she can choose.
Christina knows fulfilment
is promised,
the gates of heaven in range of her prayer.

A life for our Sister Christina –
but no perfect healing.

The second Christina (one God
but not one father) is a red-fleshed
virgin, an excellent mare.
Only the look!
The stricken look when the sun is shining.
And something not conceived
as love.
Heat comes.
Ice comes.
She labours to sleep,
our Sister Christina. All day long
in rage she drives the little Sisters –
all day long
the virgin kneels.

Suzanne is alien. If not to the mother of god,
then to herself.
When there's a tolling to prayer
from the tower,
her head flinches unknowing
as from a whip.

No!
Don't imagine
a lovelier one than Marie!
My God –
Oh God, keep
far away
the steps of my prince!

23

Irena and Olga are glorious with love.
When they sink down
together
to kiss his thin body,
rinse
his mute face with warm
tears,
my sister's frozen eyes
say:
Blessed are the crucified
thus crucified!

Our hearts invented a place,
yes, a place in the world
where we would know life without end.
Your lives, how they seize the future!
To our Sister Clarisse – the world
is a waiting-room to be prized.

Blessed the Creator! For He has
in His world: such a Sister,
such patience,
such waiting-rooms.

Most blessed of the nuns the holy flesh
already hallowed by sin.
In the grades of importance,
she is the clapper of the convent.
Not by her loud voice,
but by her great legs
towing the mystery of the world.

She knew it. In her lips –
scorched straps – it is chained,
shredded as a clothes line.
The holy flesh, our Sister!
With head thrust forward she is the first
who marches to confession
like a battering ram to a wall.
A statue could be shaped
from the stuff in her! And add a drawn sword.

She
pities my sister.
And does not like
black sheep.

Part Three

26

My sister loves the Mother Superior.
A hood covers her clear forehead,
not her shivering heart.

My sister sees the Mother Superior.
Maybe her heart shakes with too much fervour.
Maybe she also has no
place to escape.

When the sun fornicates with the invaders,
the Mother's eyes
store up the spring;

when she faces his high image
in her small
thin shape – the cross drops down.
Body to body
silent. Except for the eyes.
Maybe at the end of time we shall know whom to blame
that now such a heart
is split!

Every day Mother Superior dins hymns
in my sister.
She chants to her and does not speak.

My sister sings in another choir.

27

Oh one who commanded us to be children*
quiet
and frightened.

The day I turned back
when a black cat crossed my path!

The day I wept for the neighbour's daughter
when her bridegroom found an empty bucket!

Oh night grinding
sleep! Fear entered all my bones
– I cut my nails at the window!

Every Sunday
my window shakes from the bells of Saint Mary:
every Sunday
my heart is dumb, fearing
the dread of the deep –

Oh one who commanded us to be children
more quiet than fire.

*Oh one who commanded us: A fragmentary echo of the formula used in the traditional benediction recited before carrying out a divine commandment.

My sister sits happy
at her bridegroom's table. She does not cry.
My sister will do no such thing:
what would people say!

My sister sits happy
at her bridegroom's table. Her heart is awake.
The whole world drinks
kosher chicken soup:*

the dumplings of unleavened flour
were made by her mother-in-law. The world is amazed
and tastes the mother's confection.

My sister-bride sits. A small dish
of honey beside her. Such a huge crowd!
Father twisted
the braids of the *chalah*.†

Our father took his bread, bless God,
forty years from one oven. He never imagined
a whole people could rise in the ovens
and the world, with God's help, go on.

My sister sits at the table in her bridal veil
alone. From the hideout of mourners
the voice of a bridegroom comes near.
We will set the table without you;
the marriage contract will be written in stone.

  Kosher chicken soup ... dumplings: It was the custom among
Eastern European Jews for bride and groom to share a bowl of
clear chicken broth after the marriage ceremony.
  †The *chalah*, or twisted loaf of Sabbath bread, was part of the
festive wedding meal.

Oh one who asked for the hand of my sister.
Oh one who closed in on her in the valley
to kiss her on the mouth without witness.
With lips tasting clay
my bridegrooms,
go, look for her now.

We put her at the foot of the wall
that understands silence.
We put her on the mound
like a naked stem.
Blessed be he among men
who will bring her to his rooms,
my bridegrooms!

30
White
white
white
in white

the Dominican Convent prays:
God's estate is draped with quiet flowers,
flooded with profound salvation.
What shall we do for our sister
and she like a wilted tendril?

31

A usual morning.
The light of each separate star still
visible.
A bright point of light like an aimless balloon.
My sister
tries to catch

through the grille!
The light-moth spins off,
the window is frozen.
With a patch of muslin
from the dress of her doll
she stretches her hand for it,
does not despair.

To watch with soft eyes
the rising morning. Wipe from the lips
the taste of hot ash.
To bring back
a world to innocence,
as if to its socket a bone
from the foot of the dead.
To return there!
To the city,

and plant there again chestnut trees
in the square,
common bellflowers
near the fence,
and not to fear,
not to fear that the beating darkness
will suddenly close up your sobs
in the bars of a song.

Fragile, my sister!
My fragile sister.

33

In the whisper of chestnuts, in the foaming earth
filled with dark signs,
in the beat of the heart
like a flock of gulls bursting toward you,
in a smell of moss
in the wall,
in joy rising from fissures,
like water collected in cracks,
at the door of your home, my sister,
spring

spring
spring lords over the land!
Already dawn opens wide in the valley.
Only your angels are late.
They give no sign.
They will not say when.

Perhaps a rider will return.
Perhaps the brother.
In the woods my sister plays
hopscotch
with the messiah.

34

A tortured forest. Leaves and crown sacrificed
to a violent autumn.
Bare,
against stars of hostile brilliance,
contrived to guard tubers of spring.

My home carried its roots
to the stake.
With what –
with what, little sister,
shall we weave and draw the dream
now?

Part Four

35
i
In seventy-seven funerals we circled the wall
and the wall stood.
From the promised land I called you,
I looked for you
among heaps of small shoes.
At every approaching holiday.

No man will cure,
nor heaven,
the offence of your scalding silence.

My blessing
did not light your eyes.
My curse
came too late.

ii
– to say goodbye to you
even in one word
whispered

that you were no burden to us.
On the way.
Mother walked heavy.

I.
All your brothers.
And the desperate convoy.
Our strength did not give out,
only the earth below gave out.

iii
No entry to sheds.
On cold stoves.
When we made our beds on steaming
dung.
Before eyes wet
with rotten joy.
In the face of dogs
too proud to bark –

even when shame came into all my limbs,
with transparent nails glaring,
we clung to our flesh
as if alive.

Until we lay down our heads
one near the other.
Until we saw our faces
one within the other.
At the edge of the redeeming pit,
my sister,
we remembered your going alone.

You were not privileged to be condemned to death.
You did not enter a covenant of blood.
On the day when you will be spoken for –
behold you
are consecrated*
more than eagles
and angels.

*Behold you are consecrated: Part of the formula recited by the groom to the bride during the marriage ceremony: 'Behold you are consecrated unto me with this ring according to the law of Moses and Israel.' The previous line also alluded to a wedding, being a verbatim quotation from Song of Songs viii, 8, the verse that introduces the little sister who is to be married.

37

I vów by you today.
We will not speak, for better or for worse,
of a world that went to ruin. Oh terror –
how will this passage of our lives
be told now.

This night, only snow.
Put your face
in the path of the dogs.
Put on the dress
our mother sewed for you,
the only one
left, in white folds.

We have no other dress.
We have no other prayer.
This sun,
no other.
Let us rise up, oh sister,
your time has come!

Behold you* – behold
they.
So long as the night covers you like a canopy
let us go forth.
Say to them nicely
thank you.
Be grateful
for every hour
of refuge.
Perhaps they were not guilty –
there is always someone more guilty:
(the victim)
(the victim)
Perhaps they heard
only the voice of their hearts:

Go, they said.
Go.
My fragile sister!
You must
go.
Come, sister,
quiet.
Quiet.

*Behold you: The truncated beginning of the marriage ceremony formula, made clear by the allusion in the third line to the traditional bridal canopy under which the ceremony is conducted.

40

We knew what the hazards were –
to cross the soft earth,
to pass by the glowing iron
and to say to a stranger
– a world was here.

It comes upon me from behind
– a choir of stones
here!
In the unrepenting street of the city
the shorn head of my sister
breaks out of a wall.

sealed in a tomb
unhealed   troops of scorpions rake me
steal me out, take me   voice of my love
(door)
(door)
house of clay   house of life
undo me   renew me
(door)
(door)
my love like a deer
who finds me   who floods me   who fills me
delight when I   sorrow
my love who speaks   near now
(over)
(it's over)

*The Hebrew here imitates the peculiar style of the medieval *piyut*, or liturgical poem, with its exaggerated use of internal rhyme, alliteration, word-play, and its densely allusive quality. The key allusion here, made clear in the Hebrew through the insistence on the word *dodi*, 'my love', is to the Song of Songs. In this section, the translation has concentrated more on retaining the song-like quality than on the exact literal meaning.

Part Five

42

As the fire died. Still everyone stays,
and already everything
has gone out – the flames,
the vault of heaven,
the clothes,
and the brightness
in the eyes of those who stand off.

The noble will rush together then
to those who were burning. To throw water
on every man
– is there a stone boiling still in their hearts?

43

As in a flood dammed too late,
they will come, come to the shore,
their hearts full of pity, to set
the survivors with swollen feet
in the book of chronicles,

to extend a brother's hand!
And they gave them a hand
in spite of their ugly smell.
And before heart and reason could separate
they cried,
and applauded them.
As in a melodrama that ended:
the *characters*
are asked
to step before the curtain!

They came out.
They stretched their whole hands to the bread
still fearing hunger.
They stood.
When they smelled plates of soup,
they unwrapped tin spoons
from their leggings.
And all who came near, when they gnawed the bones,
seemed oppressors or thieves.

And they rose up.
In Europe the sun was shining,
and they
bought black umbrellas
as if they were daggers;

and while you stood trembling
I wanted to say to you,
my sister!
Tomorrow they will be the first to forget:
they will cover up my blood.

45

The Bikur Cholim Hospital
walls soaked
with the smell of sour urine
and dying hopes.

In the old hospital
among walls of red brick
my sister died.

She was two hours old. Suddenly
her eyelids contracted to look –
my sister did not scream.
She was not introduced to the world.

You are silent.
But our mother used to light
a candle for the saving of her soul*
every day.

The candles ran out in the ghetto, and the oxygen
in the shed:
my mother kindled her soul
on all the seas.

Our mother mourned a daughter
who never came into the world.
Eight years.† The rest of her sons were cut down,
and she lamented them,
and she mourned my little sister
who never came into the world.

— You who saw

everything.
You who saw us,
mother!
How mourn to our faces
someone
who never came into the world?

And the mother stared at me for a while.
And she stared at me for a long while.
Until her lips parted to speak,

A candle for the saving of her soul: An allusion to the traditional
Jewish practice, in which the mourner, during the first week of
bereavement or on the anniversary of a death, lights a candle for
the 'saving' or ascent of the departed soul.
   †*Eight years*: In the Hebrew they are specified, 1940 to 1948.

and she said, my son
– she was not privileged to see
the light of the day!

And she came close
And she prepared the candle.
And her hand was holding
another wick.

no one will carry my mother's bier with me
no one will come close to my mother's bier with me
come to the vast plains
lead your eyes to the white river
it scoops out its channel and shoves
like the prow of a heavy
ship in the ice
and say with me
imi
*imi**

imi imi: Hebrew: 'my mother, my mother', echoing the 'with me' (*imi*) of the previous line. The repeated syllables may be, among other things, a reversal of an expected, 'And say with me/ amen, amen.'

Nelly Sachs

Translated from the German by Michael Hamburger,
Ruth and Matthew Mead, and Michael Roloff

Selected by Stephen Spender

Note on the Translators

Translators are given by initials at the end of each poem and can be identified as follows:

M.H.   Michael Hamburger
R.M.M.   Ruth and Matthew Mead
M.R.   Michael Roloff

from In the Habitations of Death

For my dead brothers and sisters

O the Chimneys

And though after my skin worms destroy this
body, yet in my flesh shall I see God. JOB, xix, 26

O the chimneys
On the ingeniously devised habitations of death
When Israel's body drifted as smoke
Through the air –
Was welcomed by a star, a chimney sweep,
A star that turned black
Or was it a ray of sun?

O the chimneys!
Freedomway for Jeremiah and Job's dust –
Who devised you and laid stone upon stone
The road for refugees of smoke?

O the habitations of death,
Invitingly appointed
For the host who used to be a guest –
O you fingers
Laying the threshold
Like a knife between life and death –

O you chimneys,
O you fingers
And Israel's body as smoke through the air!

M.R.

But Who Emptied Your Shoes of Sand

But who emptied your shoes of sand
When you had to get up, to die?
The sand which Israel gathered,
Its nomad sand?
Burning Sinai sand,
Mingled with throats of nightingales,
Mingled with wings of butterflies,
Mingled with the hungry dust of serpents;
Mingled with all that fell from the wisdom of Solomon,
Mingled with what is bitter in the mystery of wormwood –

O you fingers
That emptied the deathly shoes of sand.
Tomorrow you will be dust
In the shoes of those to come.

M.H.

A Dead Child Speaks

My mother held me by my hand.
Then someone raised the knife of parting:
So that it should not strike me,
My mother loosed her hand from mine.
But she lightly touched my thighs once more
And her hand was bleeding –

After that the knife of parting
Cut in two each bite I swallowed –
It rose before me with the sun at dawn
And began to sharpen itself in my eyes –
Wind and water ground in my ear
And every voice of comfort pierced my heart –

As I was led to death
I still felt in the last moment
The unsheathing of the great knife of parting.

R.M.M.

Already embraced by the arm of heavenly solace
The insane mother stands
With the tatters of her torn mind
With the charred tinders of her burnt mind
Burying her dead child,
Burying her lost light,
Twisting her hands into urns,
Filling them with the body of her child from the air,
Filling them with his eyes, his hair from the air,
And with his fluttering heart –

Then she kisses the air-born being
And dies!

M.R.

What Secret Cravings of the Blood

What secret cravings of the blood,
Dreams of madness and earth
A thousand times murdered,
Brought into being the terrible puppeteer

Him who with foaming mouth
Dreadfully swept away
The round, the circling stage of his deed
With the ash-grey, receding horizon of fear?

O the hills of dust, which as though drawn by an evil
  moon
The murderers enacted:

Arms up and down,
Legs up and down
And the setting sun of Sinai's people
A red carpet under their feet.

Arms up and down,
Legs up and down
And on the ash-grey receding horizon of fear
Gigantic the constellation of death
That loomed like the clock face of ages.

                                        M.H.

If I Only Knew

If I only knew
On what your last look rested.
Was it a stone that had drunk
So many last looks that they fell
Blindly upon its blindness?

Or was it earth,
Enough to fill a shoe,
And black already
With so much parting
And with so much killing?

Or was it your last road
That brought you a farewell from all the roads
You had walked?

A puddle, a bit of shining metal,
Perhaps the buckle of your enemy's belt,
Or some other small augury
Of heaven?

Or did this earth,
Which lets no one depart unloved,
Send you a bird-sign through the air,
Reminding your soul that it quivered
In the torment of its burnt body?

R.M.M.

Chorus of the Rescued

We, the rescued,
From whose hollow bones death had begun to whittle
    his flutes,
And on whose sinews he had already stroked his bow –
Our bodies continue to lament
With their mutilated music.
We, the rescued,
The nooses wound for our necks still dangle
before us in the blue air –
Hourglasses still fill with our dripping blood.
We, the rescued,
The worms of fear still feed on us.
Our constellation is buried in dust.
We, the rescued,
Beg you:
Show us your sun, but gradually.
Lead us from star to star, step by step.
Be gentle when you teach us to live again.
Lest the song of a bird,
Or a pail being filled at the well,
Let our badly sealed pain burst forth again
and carry us away –
We beg you:
Do not show us an angry dog, not yet –
It could be, it could be
That we will dissolve into dust –
Dissolve into dust before your eyes.
For what binds our fabric together?
We whose breath vacated us,
Whose soul fled to Him out of that midnight
Long before our bodies were rescued
Into the ark of the moment.

We, the rescued,
We press your hand
We look into your eye –
But all that binds us together now is leave-taking,
The leave-taking in the dust
Binds us together with you.

M.R.

Chorus of the Stones

We stones
When someone lifts us
He lifts the Foretime –
When someone lifts us
He lifts the Garden of Eden –
When someone lifts us
He lifts the knowledge of Adam and Eve
And the serpent's dust-eating seduction.

When someone lifts us
He lifts in his hand millions of memories
Which do not dissolve in blood
Like evening.
For we are memorial stones
Embracing all dying.

We are a satchel full of lived life.
Whoever lifts us lifts the hardened graves of earth.
You heads of Jacob,
For you we hide the roots of dreams
And let the airy angels' ladders
Sprout like the tendrils of a bed of bindweed.

When someone touches us
He touches the wailing wall.
Like a diamond your lament cuts our hardness
Until it crumbles and becomes a soft heart –
While you turn to stone.
When someone touches us
He touches the forked ways of midnight
Sounding with birth and death.

When someone throws us –
He throws the Garden of Eden –
The wine of the stars –
The eyes of the lovers and all betrayal –

When someone throws us in anger
He throws aeons of broken hearts
And silken butterflies.

Beware, beware
Of throwing a stone in anger –
Breath once transfused our minglement,
Which grew solid in secret
But can awaken at a kiss.

R.M.M.

Chorus of the Unborn

We the unborn
The yearning has begun to plague us
The shores of blood broaden to receive us
Like dew we sink into love
But still the shadows of time lie like questions
Over our secret.

You who love,
You who yearn,
Listen, you who are sick with parting:
We are those who begin to live in your glances,
In your hands which are searching the blue air –
We are those who smell of morning.
Already your breath is inhaling us,
Drawing us down into your sleep
Into the dreams which are our earth
Where night, our black nurse,
Lets us grow
Until we mirror ourselves in your eyes
Until we speak into your ear.

We are caught
Like butterflies by the sentries of your yearning –
Like birdsong sold to earth –
We who smell of morning,
We future lights for your sorrow.

R.M.M.

The Voice of the Holy Land

O my children,
Death has run through your hearts
As through a vineyard –
Painted *Israel* red on all the walls of the world.

What shall be the end of the little holiness
Which still dwells in my sand?
The voices of the dead
Speak through reed pipes of seclusion.

Lay the weapons of revenge in the field
That they grow gentle –
For even iron and grain are akin
In the womb of earth –

But what shall be the end of the little holiness
Which still dwells in my sand?

The child murdered in sleep
Arises; bends down the tree of ages
And pins the white breathing star
That was once called Israel
To its topmost bough.
Spring upright again, says the child,
To where tears mean eternity.

R.M.M.

from Eclipse of the Stars

In memory of my father

Job

O you windrose of agonies!
Swept by primordial storms
always into other directions of inclemency;
even your South is called loneliness.
Where you stand is the navel of pain.

Your eyes have sunk deep into your skull
like cave doves which the hunter
fetches blindly at night.
Your voice has gone dumb,
having too often asked *why*.

Your voice has joined the worms and fishes.
Job, you have cried through all vigils
but one day the constellation of your blood
shall make all rising suns blanch.

M.R.

Why the Black Answer of Hate

Why the black answer of hate
to your existence, Israel?

You stranger
from a star one farther away
than the others.
Sold to this earth
that loneliness might be passed on.

Your origin entangled in weeds –
your stars bartered
for all that belongs to moths and worms,
and yet: fetched away from dreamfilled sandy shores of
    time
like moonwater into the distance.

In the others' choir
you always sang
one note lower
or one note higher –

you flung yourself into the blood of the evening sun
like one pain seeking the other.
Long is your shadow
and it has become late for you
Israel!

How far your way from the blessing
along the aeon of tears
to the bend of the road
where you turned to ashes

and your enemy with the smoke
of your burned body
engraved your mortal abandonment
on the brow of heaven!

O such a death!
When all helping angels
with bleeding wings
hung tattered
in the barbed wire of time!

Why the black answer of hate
to your existence
Israel?

                                        M.R.

Israel

Israel,
more nameless then,
still ensnared in the ivy of death,
in you eternity worked secretly, dream-deep
you mounted
the enchanted spiral of the moon towers,
circling the constellations disguised
by animal masks –
in the mute miraculous silence of Pisces
or the battering charges of Aries.

Until the sealed sky broke open
and you,
most daredevil of sleepwalkers,
fell, struck by the wound of God
into the abyss of light –

Israel,
zenith of longing,
wonder is heaped
like a storm upon your head,
breaks in your time's mountains of pain.

Israel,
tender at first, like the song of a bird
and the talk of suffering children
the source of the living God,
a native spring,
flows from your blood.

R.M.M.

In the Evening Your Vision Widens

In the evening your vision widens
looks out beyond midnight –
twofold I stand before you –
green bud rising out of dried-up sepal,
in the room where we are of two worlds.
You too already extend far beyond the dead,
those who are here,
and know of what has flowered
out of the earth with its bark of enigma.

As in the womb the unborn
with the primordial light on its brow
has the rimless view
from star to star –
So ending flows to beginning
like the cry of a swan.
We are in a sickroom.
But the night belongs to the angels.

                                        M.R.

Butterfly

What lovely aftermath
is painted in your dust.
You were led through the flaming
core of earth,
through its stony shell,
webs of farewell in the transient measure.

Butterfly
blessed night of all beings!
The weights of life and death
sink down with your wings
on the rose
which withers with the light ripening homewards.

What lovely aftermath
is painted in your dust.
What royal sign
in the secret of the air.

R.M.M.

from And No One Knows How To Go On

In the Blue Distance

In the blue distance
where the red row of apple trees wanders
– rooted feet climbing the sky –
the longing is distilled
for all those who live in the valley,

The sun, lying by the roadside
with magic wands,
commands the travellers to halt.

They stand still
in the glassy nightmare
while the cricket scratches softly
at the invisible

and the stone dancing
changes its dust to music.

R.M.M.

Then Wrote the Scribe of The Sohar

Then wrote the scribe of *The Sohar*
opening the words'. mesh of veins
instilling blood from stars
which circled, invisible, and ignited
only by yearning.

The alphabet's corpse rose from the grave,
alphabet angel, ancient crystal,
immured by creation in drops of water
that sang – and through them you saw
glinting lapis, ruby and jacinth,
when stone was still soft
and sown like flowers.

And night, the black tiger,
roared; and there tossed
and bled with sparks
the wound called day.

The light was a mouth that did not speak,
only an aura intimated the soul-god now.

M.R.

And Unwraps, As Though It Were Linen Sheets

And unwraps, as though it were linen sheets
in which birth and death are swathed,
the alphabet womb, chrysalis
of green and red and white obscurity
and swaddles it again in love-grief
as mothers do; for grief is a hiding place for light.

Yet while like summer he behaves, or winter,
yearned-for things already hover, yearnfully transformed.

M.R.

Landscape of Screams

At night when dying proceeds to sever all seams
the landscape of screams
tears open the black bandage,

Above Moria, the falling off cliffs to God,
there hovers the flag of the sacrificial knife
Abraham's scream for the son of his heart,
at the great ear of the Bible it lies preserved.

O hieroglyphs of screams
engraved at the entrance gate to death.

Wounded coral of shattered throat flutes.

O, O hands with finger vines of fear,
dug into wildly rearing manes of sacrificial blood –

Screams, shut tight with the shredded mandibles of fish,
woe tendril of the smallest children
and the gulping train of breath of the very old,

slashed into seared azure with burning tails.
Cells of prisoners, of saints,
tapestried with the nightmare pattern of throats,
seething hell in the doghouse of madness
of shackled leaps –

This is the landscape of screams!
Ascension made of screams
out of the bodies grate of bones,

arrows of screams, released
from bloody quivers.

Job's scream to the four winds
and the scream concealed in Mount Olive
like a crystal-bound insect overwhelmed by impotence.

O knife of evening red, flung into the throats
where trees of sleep rear blood-licking from the ground,
where time is shed
from the skeletons in Hiroshima and Maidanek.

Ashen scream from visionary eye tortured blind –

O you bleeding eye
in the tattered eclipse of the sun
hung up to be dried by God
in the cosmos –

M.R.

How Many Oceans Have Vanished in Sand

How many oceans have vanished in sand,
how much sand has been prayed hard in the stone,
how much time has been wept away
in the singing horn of the seashells,
how much mortal abandonment
in the fishes' pearl eyes,
how many morning trumpets in the coral,
how many star patterns in crystal,
how much seed of laughter in the gull's throat,
how many threads of longing for home
have been traversed on the nightly course of the
    constellations,
how much fertile earth
for the root of the word:
You –
behind all the crashing screens
of the secrets
You –

M.R.

from Flight and Metamorphosis

Fleeing

Fleeing,
what a great reception
on the way –

Wrapped
in the wind's shawl
feet in the prayer of sand
which can never say amen
compelled
from fin to wing
and further –

The sick butterfly
will soon learn again of the sea –
This stone
with the fly's inscription
gave itself into my hand –

I hold instead of a homeland
the metamorphoses of the world –

R.M.M.

from Journey Into a Dustless Realm

The Swan

Nothing
above the waters
and at once on the flick of an eye
is suspended
swanlike geometry
rooted in water
vining up
and bowed again
Swallowing dust
and measuring the universe
with air –

M.R.

The Ages of Night

The ages of night
are embedded in this amethyst
and an earlier intelligence of light
ignites the melancholy
which then still flowed
and wept

Your dying still shines
hard violet

R.M.M.

from Death Still Celebrates Life

The Archive Unfolded Before Me

The archive unfolded before me
in the steps of the marble stairs
the alphabet outlined
in the gills of age-old water marvels

Breath that was
petrified
and now as on lightning with feet
trampled down by us
who are burdened
and unknowingly cause
many minutes' death –

And then
disclosed in the Bible
prophesying the soul's wandering secret
and always pointing as with fingers from graves
into the next dawn –

M.R.

Thus the Mountain Climbs

Thus the mountain climbs
into my window.
Love is inhuman,
transports my heart
into the splendour of your dust.
My blood becomes a melancholy granite.
Love is inhuman.

Night and death build their land
inwards and outwards –
not for the sun.
Star is a sealed evening word –
ripped
by the inhuman upsurge
of love.

R.M.M.

from Glowing Enigmas

Part One

This night
I turned the corner into
a dark side street
Then my shadow
lay down in my arm
This tired piece of clothing
wanted to be carried
and the colour Nothing addressed me:
You are beyond!

Up and down I walk
in the room's warmth
The mad people in the corridor screech
together with the black birds outside
about the future
Our wounds blast this evil time
but slowly the clocks tick –

Doing nothing
perceptible wilting
My hands belong to a wingbeat stolen and carried off
With them I am sewing around a hole
but they sigh before this open abyss –

I wash my clothes
Much dying sings in the shift
here and there the counterpoint death
The pursuers have threaded in
together with the hypnosis
and the material absorbs it willingly in sleep –

Effulgence of lights enters into the dark verse
blows with the banner called understanding
I am to go out and search horror
Finding is elsewhere –

Behind the door
you pull on the rope of longing
till tears come
In this wellspring you're mirrored –

Here we wind a wreath
Some have violets of thunder
I have only a blade of grass
full of the silent language
that makes this air flash –

Only death draws out of them the truth of misery
these recurring rhymes cut out of night's blackness
these tongue exercises
at the end of the organ of sounds –

This telegraphy measures with the mathematics à la
    satane
the sensitively music-making places
in my body
An angel builds from the desires of love
dies and rises again in the letters
in which I travel –

If now you desperately call the one name
out of the darkness –

Wait a moment longer –
and you walk upon the sea
Already the element transfuses your pores
you are lowered with it and lifted
and found again soon in the sand
and on the stars an awaited guest arriving by air
and consumed in the fire of reunion
                                          be still – be still –

Time's pasture cropped
on the amber of your face
The night thunderstorm approaches flaming
but the rainbow
already is stretching its colours
on to the convex surface of comfort –

Those who live on have clutched at time
until gold dust was left on their hands
They sing sun – sun –
midnight the dark eye
has been covered with the shroud –

Solitude of silent velvety fields
of violas
abandoned by red and blue
violet the going colour
your weeping creates it
from the delicate fear of your eyes –

You have misplaced your name
but the world comes running
to offer you a good selection
You shake your head
but your lover
once found your needle for you in a haystack
Listen – he's calling already –

The beds are being made for pain
The linen is pain's close friend
It wrestles with the archangel
who never discards his invisibility
Breath weighed down with stones looks for new ways
   out
but the crucified star
falls again and again like windfalls
on to pain's shawl –

When I come to leave the room protected by illness
free to live – to die –
air with its welcoming kiss
deeply delights the twin mouth
then I shall not know
what my invisible
will do with me now –

You speak with me in the night
but fought off like all the dead
you have left the last letter
and the music of throats
to earth
that sings farewell up and down all the scales
But bedded in the blown sand
I hear new sounds in grace –

Princesses of sadness
who fishes out your sorrows?
Where do the funerals take place?
What ocean straits weep for you
with the embrace of an inner homeland?

Night your sister
takes leave of you
as the last lover –

Forgive me my sisters
I have taken your silence into my heart
There it lives and suffers the pearls of your suffering
heartache knocks
so loud so piercingly shrill
A lioness rides on the waves of Oceana
a lioness of pains
that long ago gave her tears to the sea –

Quickly death is removed from sight
The elements riot
but the budding spheres
already press in with resurrection
and that which is wordless heals the ailing star –

Weep away the unleashed heaviness of fear
Two butterflies support the weight of the world for you
and I lay your tears into these words:
Your fear has begun to shine –

In one moment a star closes its eye
The toad loses its moonstone
You in your bed give your breath to night
O map of the universe
Your signs show the veins of strangeness
out of our minds –

Disinherited we weep for dust –

My love flowed out into your martyrdom
broke through death
We live in resurrection –

In the bewitched wood
with the peeled-off bark of existence
where footprints bleed
glowing enigmas gaze at each other
intercept messages
from grave vaults –

Behind them
appears the second vision
the secret pact has been made –

Sick people are about to recapture
wild beasts that broke out of their blood –
Going out to hunt with their eyes
to that place where day
lies in colours startled by death
and the depth of the moon
enters their wide-open hibernation
sharply drawing them upward
until the thread of earth breaks
and they hang on the snow apple
their limbs beating –
My beloved dead
a hair made of darkness even
is called remoteness
softly grows through open time
I die filling a secret measure
into the minute

that budding stretches
but behind my back they have planted
the tongues of fire on to the earth –
A vine that yields its juice to the flame
I sink back –

As I wait here
time yearns out at sea
but is pulled back again and again by its blue hair
does not reach eternity –
Still no love between the planets
but a secret understanding already quivers –

A bleeding away wide as the evening
till darkness digs the grave
embryo of the dream in the womb
knocks
Creative air slowly covers itself
with the skin of new birth
Pain inscribes itself
with the fan of visions
life and death go on –

New Flood again and again
with those letters brought out by torture
those fishes that speak on the hook
in the skeleton of salt
to make legible the wound –

To learn dying again and again
from the old life
flight through the door of air
to fetch new sin from sleeping planets
Extreme exercise upon the old element of breathing

startled by new death
What became of the tear
when earth vanished?

They speak snow –
The cloth of hours with its four cosmic ends
bears itself in
war and flight to the stars crouch next to each other
look for asylum where night
overflows with mother's milk
and beckons with a black finger
where new discoveries await the soul explorers
sparkling in darkness
deep underneath the snow –

M.H.

Part Three

In my room
where my bed stands
a table a chair
the kitchen stove
the universe kneels as everywhere
to be redeemed
from invisibility –
I draw a line
write down the alphabet
paint on the wall the suicidal words
that make the newborn burgeon at once
I have just fastened the planets to truth
when the earth begins to hammer
night works loose
drops out
dead tooth from the gum –

This is an excursion to a place
where the shadows sign other contracts –
you sit turned away from me
your back moves through night
your talk with the other side is mute
prophecies – pale lightning
on the wall of ashes
There's much dying out there in the greenness
You are sandy nearness out there in your graves

And you walked over death
like a bird in snow
always blackly sealing the end –
Time gulped down
whatever you gave it of parting
right to the utmost forsaking
along the fingertips
night of eyes
To grow bodiless
The air was washed all round by –
an ellipse – the street of pains –

Then alone
with the shivering wing
like men in polar ice
where always there is a supernumerary One –
the mourning-cloak night
has a wound
won't cover me –

Am in strange parts
protected by the 8
the holy looped angel
He is always on his way

through our flesh
creating unrest
and making dust ripe for flying –

And I think of her
in the delirium of falling
whose child re-created her out of air
'your right leg bird-light –
your left leg bird-light –
tooee tooee –
Call in the south wind
Hearts like water can tremble in one's hand
like water tremble
Eyelid held open by depth –'

I saw him step from the house
the fire had singed
but not burned him
He carried a briefcase of sleep
under one arm
heavy inside with letters and figures
a whole arithmetic –
Into his arm was branded:
7337 the ruling number
These numbers had conspired among themselves
The man was a surveyor
Already his feet were rising from the earth
One was waiting for him above
to build a new paradise
'Only wait – you too will soon be at rest –'

Captive everywhere
the street that I walk
the vehicles I avoid

Put away the things I have bought
all visionary excursions into your realms –
My foot trips – hurts
a detour into your dwellings –

Deborah was stabbed by stars
and yet sang triumphant hymns
when the mountains dissolved
and on white-gleaming donkeys like prophets
the troop of horsemen moved on

But silence is where the victims dwell –

A game like blindman's buff
on the green meadow
when the virgins pursued
hunted by deadly panic
climbed on to trees
that grew into the sky
and they plunged into the void
the sevenfold constellation
lost the tear
in the orphans' colony –

Who can hide
like a river in the sea
or bend night
brazenly sleeping
into the white fire
that writes 'Open'
when earth is five inches of misery
beneath her creator –

Not HERE nor THERE
but double-tongued in sleep
Nature stammers out her decline
the shadow goes home
The planet rambles along the lines of life
sucking in regal messages
grows richer –

They collided in the street
Two destinies on this earth
Two circulations of blood in their arteries
Two that breathed on their way
in this solar system
Over their faces a cloud passed
time had cracked
Remembrance peered in
The far and the near had fused
From past and future
two destinies glittered
and fell apart –

Leave without looking back –
tear the last quaking-grass from your eyes
When Tsong-kha-pa left his master
he did not turn to look
Departure dwelt in his stride
Time flared up from his shoulders –

The man left behind cried out:
'Throw his hovel into the chasm –'
And the hovel floated above the chasm
shot through with five-hued light –
And he of no parting strode
into the cropped place that is pure spirit

And his house was no longer a house
Only light –

Faster time faster
when the second second forces the first to its knees
the golden army all day long on the march
in haste
till at evening all have been beaten
a rosemary bush the sky
night washes death down to its primal colour
the elements sick with nostalgia break loose

run to the sea
grow breathless
refuse to blossom
for another has died
who took time's measure –

I write you –
You have come into the world again
with the haunting strength of letters
that groped for your essence
Light shines
and your fingertips glow in the night
Constellation at the birth
of darkness like these verses –

Pull over oneself
sleep the blanket of the seven sleepers
Hide with seals
that in the wound which was exiled
and ram-lightning of the Last Judgement –

But only the word lashed bloody
breaks into resurrection
the soul on its wing –

Dark hissing of the wind
in the corn
The victim ready to suffer
The roots are still
but the ears of corn
know many native languages –

And the salt in the sea
weeps afar
The stone is a fiery being
and the elements tug on their chains
to be united
when the ghostly script of the clouds
fetches home primal images

Mystery on the border of death
'Lay a finger upon your lips:
Silence Silence Silence' –

Four days four nights
a coffin was your hiding place
Survival breathed in – breathed out –
to delay death –
Between four boards
lay the world's anguish –
Outside grew the minute full of flowers
over the sky clouds played –

Thrown the seed grain's mystery
already strikes root in the future
begins:
A dance in the Ardennes
subterranean seeking
for the face in the rock crystal
Dawn in the Nothingness above
the South Sea
Lovers
hold to their ears the conch
with the deep-sea concert
A star opens to an entrance
The moon has had visitors
The old man does not return
A birth sucks at life –

M.H.

More about Penguins

Penguinews, which appears every month, contains details of all the new books issued by Penguins as they are published. From time to time it is supplemented by *Penguins in Print*, which is a complete list of all available books published by Penguins. (There are well over three thousand of these.)

A specimen copy of *Penguinews* will be sent to you free on request, and you can become a subscriber for the price of the postage. For a year's issues (including the complete lists) please send 30p if you live in the United Kingdom, or 60p if you live elsewhere. Just write to Dept EP, Penguin Books Ltd, Harmondsworth, Middlesex, enclosing a cheque or postal order, and your name will be added to the mailing list.

Note: *Penguinews* and *Penguins in Print* are not available in the U.S.A. or Canada

A Penguin Classic

The Jewish Poets of Spain

Translated by David Goldstein

Ha-Levi's yearning for the land of Israel, Gabirol's communion with his own soul, Moses ibn Ezra's grief in his exile, and the extraordinary martial character of Samuel ha-Nagid, Vizier to the Moorish king of Granada: each of these poets is represented in this anthology of Hebrew verse in Spain from the tenth to the thirteenth centuries. Their subjects range from a wine-feast in a beautiful hanging garden to the arcane treasures of immortality; and they bring together two strands of the civilization of the Jews, one the unbridled sensuality of the Song of Songs, the other the unshakable faith of the Prophets.

Poem into Poem
World Poetry in Modern Verse Translation

Edited by George Steiner

Poem into Poem is the first book of its kind. In an anthology of verse translations from twenty-two languages (ranging from ancient Hebrew and Greek to modern Chinese), each one has been made by an English or American poet who not only renders the original but also creates what is a living poem in its own right.

We find extraordinary encounters – Hardy and Sappho, Hopkins and Horace, Yeats and Ronsard, Scott Fitzgerald and Rimbaud, James Joyce and Gottfried Keller, Ezra Pound and Sophocles. The light of another poem is caught in a live mirror.

George Steiner believes that translation is central to the nature of modern poetry; that ours is the most brilliant period of poetic translation and recapture since the Elizabethans. This anthology contains his evidence.

Not for sale in the U.S.A. or Canada